Bilingual Edition

Edición Bilingüe

Let's Draw a Fish with Triangles

Vamos a dibujar un pez usando triángulos

Kathy Kuhtz Campbell
Illustrations by Emily Muschinske

Traduccion al español:
María Cristina Brusca

The Rosen Publishing Group's
PowerStart Press™ & Editorial Buenas Letras™
New York

Published in 2004 by The Rosen Publishing Group, Inc.
29 East 21st Street, New York, NY 10010

First Edition

Book Design: Emily Muschinske

Photo Credits: Pp. 23, 24 Kennan Ward/CORBIS.

Library of Congress Cataloging-in-Publication Data

Campbell, Kathy Kuhtz.
   Let's draw a fish with triangles = Vamos a dibujar un pez usando triangulos / Kathy Kuhtz Campbell ; translated by Marisa Cristina Brusca ; illustrations by Emily Muschinske.— 1st ed.
      p. cm. — (Let's draw with shapes)
English and Spanish.
Includes index.
Summary: Offers simple instructions for using triangles to draw a fish.
   ISBN 1-4042-7505-3 (library binding)
   1. Fishes in art—Juvenile literature. 2. Triangle in art—Juvenile literature. 3. Drawing—Technique—Juvenile literature. [1. Fishes in art. 2. Triangle in art. 3. Drawing—Technique. 4. Spanish language materials—Bilingual.] I. Title: Vamos a dibujar un pez usando triangulos. II. Muschinske, Emily, ill. III. Title. IV. Series.
   NC655.C3583 2004
   743.6'7—dc21
                                        2003009130

Manufactured in the United States of America

Due to the changing nature of Internet links, PowerKids Press has developed an online list of Web sites related to the subject of this book. This site is updated regularly. Please use this link to access the list:

http://www.buenasletraslinks.com/ldwsh/pez

2

Contents

1 The Top of Your Fish   4

2 The Tail   12

3 The Eye   18

Words to Know   24

Colors   24

Index   24

Contenido

1 El cuerpo de tu pez   4

2 La cola   12

3 El ojo   18

Palabras que debes saber   24

Colores   24

Índice   24

Draw a red triangle for the top of your fish.

Dibuja un triángulo rojo para hacer el cuerpo de tu pez.

5

Add an orange triangle to the body of your fish.

Agrega un triángulo anaranjado al cuerpo de tu pez.

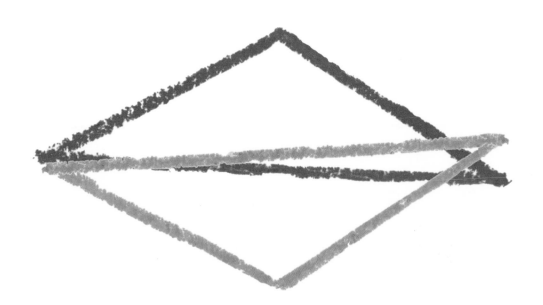

7

Add a small yellow triangle
to the top of your fish.

Agrega un pequeño
triángulo amarillo al
cuerpo de tu pez.

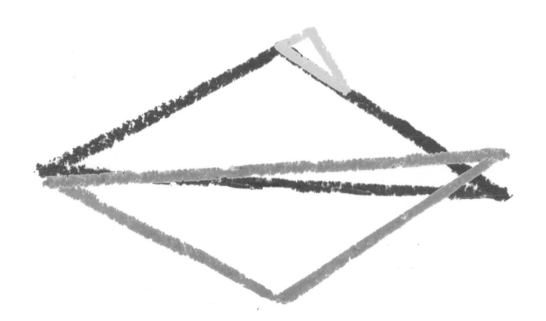

9

Add three small green
triangles to the body of
your fish.

Agrega tres pequeños
triángulos verdes al
cuerpo de tu pez.

Draw a blue triangle for the top of the tail.

Dibuja un triángulo azul para hacer una parte de la cola.

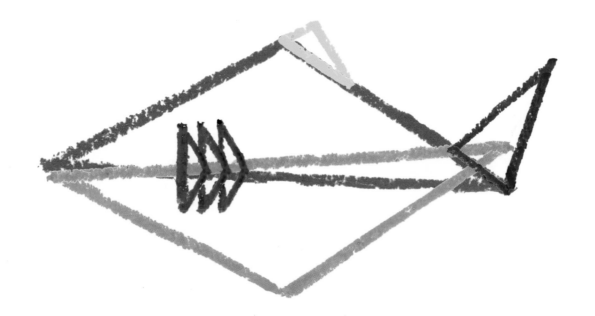

Add a purple triangle to the
tail of your fish.

Agrega un triángulo
violeta a la cola de tu pez.

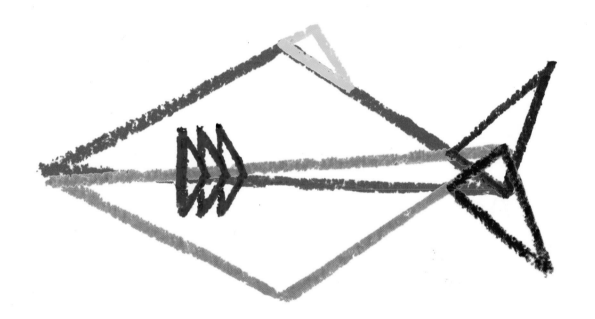

15

Add a small pink triangle to the body of the fish.

Agrega un pequeño triángulo rosa al cuerpo de tu pez.

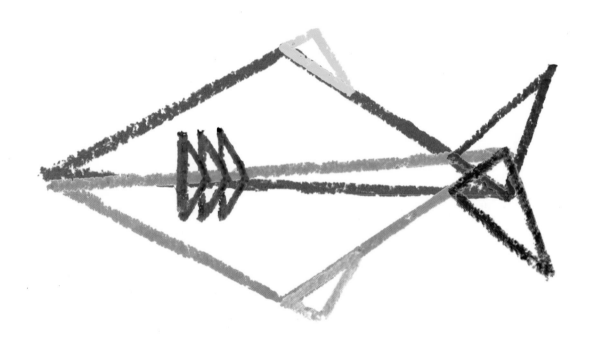

17

Draw a small black triangle
for the eye of your fish.

Dibuja un pequeño
triángulo negro para
hacer el ojo de tu pez.

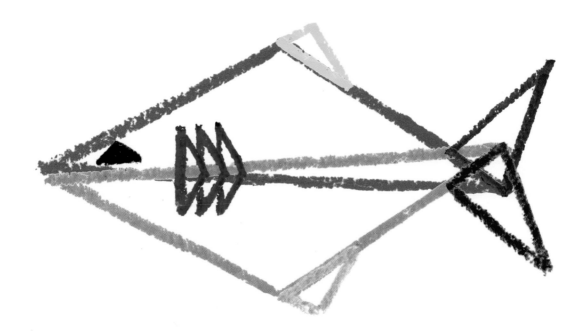

19

Color in your fish.

Colorea tu pez.

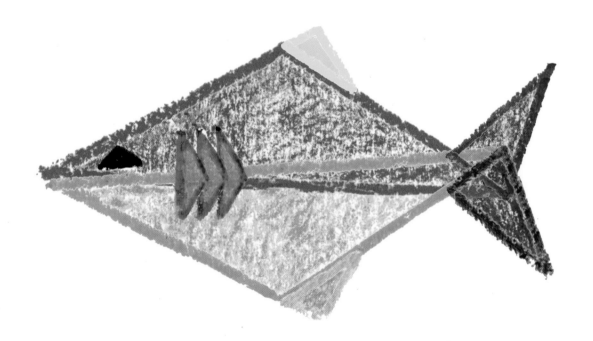

21

A fish uses its tail to help it swim in the water.

El pez usa su cola para ayudarse a nadar en el agua.

23

Words to Know
Palabras que debes saber

body
cuerpo

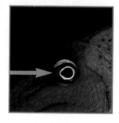
eye
ojo

tail
cola

Colors
Colores

red / rojo
orange / anaranjado
yellow / amarillo
green / verde

blue / azul
purple / violeta
pink / rosa
black / negro

Index

B
body, 6, 10, 16

C
color, 20

E
eye, 18

T
tail, 12, 14, 22

Índice

C
cola, 12, 14, 22
colorea, 20
cuerpo, 4, 6, 8,
   10, 16

O
ojo, 18

24